BASEBALL HALL OF FAMERS OF THE NEGRO LEAGUES

MONTE IRVIN

Katie Haegele

the rosen publishing group's
rosen
central

To Mom and Pop and the summer of baseball

Published in 2002 by The Rosen Publishing Group, Inc.
29 East 21st Street, New York, NY 10010

First Edition

Library of Congress Cataloging-in-Publication Data

Haegele, Katie.
Monte Irvin / Katie Haegele.— 1st ed.
p. cm. — (Baseball Hall of Famers of the Negro Leagues.)
Includes bibliographical references (p.) and index.
Summary: A description of the life of the outstanding baseball player who started in the Negro Leagues, overcame racial discrimination to play with the New York Giants, and was elected to the Baseball Hall of Fame in 1973.
ISBN 0-8239-3477-2 (lib. bdg.)
1. Irvin, Monte, 1919-—Juvenile literature. 2. Baseball players—United States—Biography—Juvenile literature. 3. African American baseball players—Biography—Juvenile literature. 4. Negro leagues—History—Juvenile literature. [1. Irvin, Monte, 1919- 2. Baseball players. 3. African Americans—Biography. 4. Negro leagues.]
I. Title. II. Series.
GV865.I78 H34 2002
796.357'092—dc21

2001003350

Manufactured in the United States of America

Contents

Monte Irvin's accomplishments in the Negro leagues landed him a spot on the roster of the New York Giants. He was one of the first players involved in the integration of major league baseball.

Introduction

Baseball has always been called the "national pastime," and during its heyday in the 1930s and 1940s, that's exactly what it was. Sports such as basketball and football, which are so popular today, were nothing compared to baseball during its golden age. Every major U.S. city had a team; every small town had local baseball clubs; and every man, woman, and child rooted their home team on to victory. Families attended games for the price of a quarter—a nickel more for a hot dog—or gathered around the radio to listen to the games on summer evenings the way people watch television together today.

The sport was something that all Americans had in common. But one of the great dividing lines in American culture kept everyone from being a part of the game. African American players had been effectively shut out of the major leagues since 1868—the earliest days of the professional sport. And baseball was far from being the only institution that showed such blatant racism.

During segregation, many African American children participated in the national pastime in abandoned lots and fields, using whatever equipment they could get their hands on.

In 1892, a man named Homer Plessy—who was one-eighth African American by heritage—was jailed for sitting on a train car reserved for white people only. Plessy argued that this rule was a violation of his civil rights, but a judge found him guilty of breaking the law. This defeat in 1896 was the beginning of the concept of "separate but equal"—the idea that African Americans and whites should use separate bathrooms, separate train cars, and separate seating areas on buses and in restaurants. Dividing African Americans and whites—whether or not the separation is equal—is known as segregation.

As a result, for many years even the most talented African American athletes were not allowed to play in the major leagues. In 1920, a man named Rube Foster started a league just for African American players. Playing ball in yards and on the street was one of the few outlets for African American kids growing up during that time, and many had grown into superior baseball players. The most gifted of the young men who learned baseball this way were the first to be signed to the Negro leagues, whose teams operated on a shoestring budget and played everywhere they could—parking lots, fields, even prison yards. Although Negro league players were as talented as white major league players, they often weren't allowed to play in the same stadiums or use the same equipment.

Foster was applying the concept of "separate but equal" to baseball when he founded the Negro leagues. But the truth is that conditions for African American players were not equal to those of white players. When Babe Ruth signed his contract in 1930, he was agreeing to $80,000 a season—an unheard-of sum for the times and an even higher salary than President Herbert Hoover's. Yet the average African American player earned only $300 a month. African Americans couldn't get the fame and money that the best white players got. But nobody could stop these men from playing the game they were born to play.

Monford "Monte" Irvin came into the world just in time to play an important role in African American baseball and American history. He was born in 1919 to a poor Alabama farming family, but the Irvins knew Monte would have a future much less humble than his beginnings. A gifted athlete, he was an all-state player in football, basketball, and baseball in high school. He even set a state record for throwing the javelin. At thirteen, just after his family had moved to New Jersey, Monte joined the local African American baseball team, the Orange Triangles. He and his brother, Bob, who was also an excellent ballplayer, proved to be a fearsome duo for the Triangles. When Monte Irvin was just seventeen, he was spotted by a talent scout and signed to play for the Negro leagues.

Racism was not the only obstacle in Monte Irvin's life. He also overcame serious illness as a teenager. In addition, just when the Negro leagues were being formed, the Great Depression flattened America and the rest of the world. Tough economic times across the country meant that most Americans couldn't afford to attend the baseball games they loved so much.

Negro league baseball was a point of pride in the African American community, and was an excuse for people to dress up and enjoy themselves even during the tough times of the Depression. It has been said that Negro league games were faster, more entertaining, and were often more exciting than the majors, and their players were all as good as or better than the white players in the major leagues. Times were not always easy, and the achievements of the best African American players is a testament to their extraordinary talent. Monte Irvin's story, just like the story of the Negro leagues themselves, is one of struggle and success.

Life Before Professional Baseball

In many ways, Monte Irvin's early life reflected the hardships taking place in America at that time. He was born with such extraordinary talent, however, that he was able to experience things most people only dream of doing.

Born on February 25, 1919, to Alabama sharecroppers, Irvin was one of thirteen children. Haleburg, Alabama, was such a tiny town in farm country that Irvin and his brothers and sisters usually told people they came from the larger town of Columbia. Irvin's given name was actually Hubert, but his older sister, Eulalia, never liked the name and took to calling him Monford. When Irvin was eight years old, his parents officially changed his name to Monford Merrill, and he went by the nickname Monty. (Years later, he would change the spelling to Monte because the "y" always dropped down onto other players' names when he signed autographs.)

Even before the Depression, Irvin's parents didn't have a lot of money. But the family was

Job seekers during the Great Depression put signs on their cars that indicated they were looking for work.

very happy and close-knit, hard-working and rarely wanting for anything. On Christmas the children looked forward to getting oranges and candy canes—not a lot of expensive presents.

A Baseball Family

Before television, the Internet, and video games, people had a different idea of entertainment. When Monte Irvin was growing up, going to a baseball game was a very exciting way to spend an afternoon, especially during the Depression, when it was a treat. Baseball was known as the national pastime

Cost of Items During the Depression:

Table Lamp	$1
Pound of Bacon	13¢
Electric Washing Machine	$33.50
Gas Stove	$19.95
Wool sweater	$1
Bottle of shampoo	25¢

Average Weekly Wages:

	Depression	Now
Factory Worker	$16.89	$500
Cook	$15	$236
Doctor	$61.11	$1,800
Accountant	$45	$700

because men and women of all ages, races, and classes loved it.

Irvin says he was fortunate to come from a "baseball family." In his town, the men and boys would work half a day on Saturday and then spend the afternoon playing baseball in a nearby field using slipshod but solid equipment: balls made of rocks wrapped in old socks, taped-up old bats. Those who had seen touring teams play knew the rules and organized the games. Monte's older brother, Bob, was also a great player, and they both worked hard and ate a lot to get big and strong.

Irvin's father, Cupid, was a farmer. As a sharecropper, he shared farmland with another man, but the man was dishonest and cheated the Irvins whenever he could. In that era, since the man was white, he could get away with mistreating the African American farmers. Cupid Irvin wanted to protect his family, but to speak up could have meant real trouble. Instead, in the spring of 1927, he found a way for his family to get out of the South. His sister, Pearl, had moved to New Jersey already, and Cupid began making plans to start a new life there.

Monte Irvin has said he can still remember the amount of money his parents needed to raise in order to afford train fare up north. All of the people in their community helped them get together the $37.10 it cost for the whole family to take the train to New Jersey!

Through all these struggles the Irvins remained close, and Cupid and his wife, Mary Eliza, believed in all of their children—especially Monte, who showed great promise as an athlete at an early age.

A Young Athlete

It was in his new hometown of Orange, New Jersey, that eight-year-old Monte developed a love for baseball. There was a park in nearby East Orange called Grove Street Oval that often hosted touring African American baseball teams. Irvin first visited the park as a young boy, and he said watching these great players was a favorite activity of everyone in the community, especially as the hard times of the Depression made more expensive entertainment unaffordable for many.

Roy Campanella, one of African American baseball's greatest players, was a lifelong friend of Irvin's. Campanella began catching for the Baltimore Elites when he was just fifteen years

Monte Irvin (*left*) congratulates Roy Campanella of the Brooklyn Dodgers on winning the National League Most Valuable Player award for 1951.

Roy Campanella

Roy Campanella ("Campy" to his friend Monte Irvin) was the first catcher to break major league baseball's color line. Born in Philadelphia to a black mother and an Italian father, Campanella joined his hometown semiprofessional team, the Bacharach Giants, in 1937. He played so well as a teenager on that team that the Baltimore Elite Giants, a Negro National League team, offered him a spot—at the age of fifteen! He started by playing part-time, and was eventually one of the best players in the Negro National League. Campanella was voted the Most Valuable Player in the 1941 East-West all-star game and played for the Mexican league for part of 1942 and all of 1943.

Making the Brooklyn Dodgers in 1948 catapulted Campanella's career to new heights. For nine years, he was the catcher for the amazing team known as "the Boys of Summer," who won National League pennants in 1949, 1952, 1953, 1955, and 1956, and gave Brooklyn its only World Series win, in 1955. Campanella himself won the MVP award three times in five years, batted .312, and scored 103 runs in 1953. His 142 RBIs led the league, and 41 home runs set major league records for catchers. Roy Campanella was elected to the Baseball Hall of Fame in 1969.

old. He and his teammates used to go to the Irvins' quite often to enjoy Mary Eliza's delicious dinners. So, even before he was a professional player, Monte Irvin had some of his baseball heroes right in his living room!

Monte Irvin was a born athlete. He excelled at every sport he tried. He was even a whiz at marbles, Ping-Pong, and swimming before he got older and wanted to concentrate on just a few sports.

At thirteen he joined the Orange Triangles, the African American baseball team in his town. He practiced every position and was soon playing them equally well. Playing on integrated teams (teams of mixed races) was something Irvin got used to at a very early age: Orange boasted a church league, a semiprofessional league, and a suburban league. This experience probably helped prepare Irvin for his future in the majors as much as practicing hitting and fielding. Other famous Negro leaguers like Roy Campanella and Jackie Robinson, who were born in the South and raised in the North, started their early careers on integrated high school teams.

In high school, Irvin began to play in earnest and developed a reputation as an all-around athlete. In fact, he earned a total of sixteen varsity letters in a variety of sports. One of those sports was track, in which he threw the

Portrait of a young Monte Irvin

discus, the shotput, and the javelin. He showed such promise in javelin that his coach encouraged him to consider training for the Olympics. One year, Irvin set the state record at 192 feet, 8 inches—a record that remained unbroken in the state of New Jersey until nearly sixty years later.

The groundwork Irvin laid by throwing the javelin in high school had a big payoff once he

W. E. B. Du Bois

W. E. B. Du Bois was one of the most influential African American leaders of the early twentieth century.

W. E. B. Du Bois was a very influential African American intellectual, scholar, and political thinker. He advocated civil rights for African Americans through social and political action and helped found the NAACP, the National Association for the Advancement of Colored People. Du Bois opposed segregation in all its forms, and disagreed with another prominent African American activist of the time, Booker T. Washington, about how to better the African American situation.

Washington thought it best to accept discrimination for the time being and urged African Americans to focus on working hard to gain the respect of white people. But Du Bois believed that social change could be accomplished by developing an elite group of college-educated African Americans he called the "Talented Tenth."

started playing professional baseball. He soon developed a reputation as a power hitter, and his throwing arm couldn't be beat. In his auto-biography, *Nice Guys Finish First,* Irvin remembers his first season with the Newark Eagles in the Negro leagues:

> I could throw so well that I used to put on exhibitions. Down at Ruppert Stadium, we sometimes had a throwing contest before the game . . . We would get way out, about three hundred feet, and hop the ball in to see who could come the closest to home plate. In one contest, on my second throw, the ball hopped behind the pitcher's mound and hit the heart of home plate for a perfect strike. Biz Mackey was the catcher and he told the other guys, "There's not any use in you guys throwing. There's no way you can beat perfection." I won that prize real easy.

Even though he took letters in four sports and enjoyed them all, the obvious choice for Monte Irvin was baseball. In his autobiography he explained: "At that time if you had any intention of playing sports, you automatically thought about baseball." In addition to playing for the Triangles, Irvin joined the Paterson Smart Set, managed by Charlie Jamieson, at Paterson East Side Park Club. Jamieson had been in the major leagues until 1932 and had even played in the 1920 World Series with the Cleveland Indians. With Jamieson's club, Irvin got the chance to play in front of crowds of three or four thousand and against both African American and white teams.

A Health Scare

Irvin's fledging career was almost stopped in its tracks by what happened during his senior year of high school. One day on his way home from school, he was struck by an unusually fierce headache. By the time he made it home he felt worse, and his mother called the family doctor, who immediately admitted him to the hospital.

It was determined that Monte had contracted a serious infection after cutting himself on the basketball court and that, instead of healing, the infection had traveled to his chest. He ended up spending months in the hospital after an operation that saved his life.

His prognosis wasn't always so positive, though. When he first arrived at the hospital, doctors didn't hold out much hope for his recovery and even asked his mother if they could amputate his infected left arm. She told them not to do it because baseball was his whole life, and if he woke up to find he could no longer play, he'd die anyway. During this time, Irvin lost a lot of blood—so much blood, in fact, that the hospital advertised in the newspaper for donations. Many students from Irvin's high school saw the ad and turned up at the hospital right away to help. As Irvin wrote in his autobiography, "They were German, Irish, and black, so I've got all kinds of blood in my veins."

Slowly but surely, Irvin got healthy again. He attributed his recovery to those kind donations, fresh air, and his mother's cooking. He was back on his feet and stronger than ever.

Segregation and the Formation of the Negro Leagues

During its heyday, baseball was a sport that gave pride and joy to Americans. But at the same time one of the great dividing lines in the national landscape kept some Americans from being a part of the action. African American players had been effectively shut out of the major leagues since 1868—the earliest professional days of the sport. All of this may seem hard to imagine now, but in fact such racist rules were the norm in America until the Civil Rights movement of the 1960s. Even after slavery was abolished in the 1860s, many laws were put into place to keep African Americans and whites from associating with one another, and also to

For a brief period between the end of slavery and the beginning of the Jim Crow era, some major league baseball teams were integrated. Moses Fleetwood Walker *(middle left)* and his brother Weldy *(top right)* both played for the Toledo Blue Stockings.

prevent African Americans from enjoying many rights white people took for granted.

The beginning of such laws was in 1865, when Black Codes were instituted in the South after the Civil War. These codes regulated civil and legal rights—everything from whom African Americans could marry to what property they could own or sell. Within a year, the codes were deemed unfair by the federal government.

Yet, in 1896, the U.S. Supreme Court introduced the concept of "separate but equal" to the American mindset with its decision in the case of *Plessy v. Ferguson.* In 1892, a thirty-year-old shoemaker named Homer Plessy refused to leave the "white" car of the East Louisiana Railroad and was thrown in jail. Plessy was one-eighth African American and seven-eighths white, but under Louisiana law, he was considered African American and was required to sit in the "colored" car. Plessy went to court and argued that the Separate Car Act violated the Thirteenth and Fourteenth Amendments to the United States Constitution.

The judge ruled that the government had the right to regulate railroad companies that operated only within Louisiana.

This decision made way for many "Jim Crow" laws, which governed the ins and outs of how people of different races could interact in public. The laws were extremely restrictive of African Americans' rights, and covered everything from eating in restaurants and using public restrooms to marriage and employment. By 1914, the laws had created two separate societies in the South—one African American, one white. Although African Americans were technically permitted to vote and hold the same jobs as whites, high poll taxes and unfair literacy tests kept them locked out of opportunities.

The Negro Leagues

In a so-called gentleman's agreement in 1868, the National Association of Base Ball Players (which later became the National League) voted to bar

During the Jim Crow era, African American students were taught in overcrowded, ill-equipped classrooms—conditions that civil rights leaders described as being separate but not equal.

Jim Crow Laws by State

Some of the following laws were in place until civil rights legislation ended segregation between 1964 and 1968:

Alabama: "It shall be unlawful for a negro and white person to play together or in company with each other at any game of pool or billiards."

Florida: "All marriages between a white person and a negro, or between a white person and a person of negro descent to the fourth generation inclusive, are hereby forever prohibited."

Georgia: "No colored barber shall serve as a barber [to] white women or girls."

Georgia: "It shall be unlawful for any amateur white baseball team to play baseball on any vacant lot or baseball diamond within two blocks of a playground devoted to the Negro race, and it shall be unlawful for any amateur colored baseball team to play baseball in any vacant lot or baseball diamond within two blocks of any playground devoted to the white race."

Mississippi: "Separate schools shall be maintained for the children of the white and colored races."

— Compiled by the Martin Luther King Jr. National Historic Site Interpretive Staff "any club which may be composed of one or more colored persons." But when the sport attained professional status the following season, pro teams were not expected to follow the rule, which after all had been set forth by an amateur association. In fact, during the nineteenth century, African Americans played on racially mixed teams, and brothers Moses Fleetwood Walker and Wilberforce "Weldy" Walker made it to the majors.

Yet the association soon clamped down and adopted the "color line" rule that had kept African American men out of the National Association of Base Ball Players. Even the most talented African American athletes couldn't play in the major leagues. This exclusion meant that for a long time African American players couldn't get the fame and salaries that the best white players received.

Still, African American players sought out ways to improve their skills. Small community and amateur leagues around the country were ground zero for some of the best baseball talent. Many loosely organized African American teams formed leagues that were known collectively as the Negro leagues. One of the best known was the Negro National League, which was formed in 1920. Another, the Eastern Colored League, was formed in 1923, and subsequently the two leagues met in a World Series every year from 1924 to 1927.

Rube Foster is sometimes called the father of African American baseball. By founding the Negro National League, he contributed to a very important part of both African American and baseball history. Three years later, Ed Bolden started the Eastern Colored League. There were actually several African American professional and semiprofessional teams during this time, but for the next ten years or so, the teams in these two leagues were on top.

When Foster started the Negro National League, he was working from the concept of separate but athletically equal. The formation of this league was by its very nature a reaction to segregation. But Foster and other leaders of African American baseball believed their

Rube Foster

Rube Foster, founder of the Negro National League

Andrew "Rube" Foster was a talented player who was able to use his baseball and business smarts in other ways. Originally chosen to pitch for the Giants, the team ended up not having space for him and took him on as a teacher for the other players. It is said that Christy Mathewson's famous "fadeaway" pitch (now called a screwball) was a trick that Foster taught him.

Foster is often considered the father of African American baseball. In 1920, he organized the first real African American major league, the Negro National League. During his time as president of the NNL, he invented the bunt-and-run and was known as a strict leader: He once cracked a player on the head with his pipe for not making the play he was told! White major leaguers often attended his games to learn his tactics. He was inducted into the Baseball Hall of Fame in 1981.

actions would accomplish a major goal of many African Americans of the time: to prove that they were equal to whites.

The Negro leagues were one example of educator Booker T. Washington's idea of African American "self-help" toward the eventual realization of an integrated world. Booker Taliaferro Washington was born a slave on a small farm in the Virginia backcountry, but went on to become one of the foremost black educators of the late nineteenth and early twentieth centuries. He also had a major influence on southern race relations and was the dominant figure in African American public affairs.

Washington believed that blacks should accept discrimination because they were powerless to change it. He wanted blacks to earn the respect of white people through submission and hard work. He believed that once African Americans proved they were equal to whites, they could achieve what he considered their highest goal: integration.

Rube Foster said that he wanted to free African Americans to pursue the sport of baseball without being under white rule, and that he was setting out to "do something concrete for the loyalty of the race."

African American baseball was a strong political and social statement, and a point of pride for African Americans of all backgrounds. According to Newark Eagles co-owner Effa Manley, everybody looked forward to the games and turned out in style: "Oh boy, did they dress. People came out who didn't know the ball from the bat. All the girls got new outfits."

Monte Irvin said that to appreciate African American baseball fully, it is important to understand the kind of world he and his fellow African Americans lived in during this time.

Negro league baseball was an important social event for African Americans

"Many of the people who came out to the ball park caught hell all week," he explained in his autobiography. "If they had a job, it was usually a menial [low-level] one, and they were not getting any encouragement at the workplace. But on Saturday or Sunday, they went to a game and saw players the same color performing well on the baseball diamond. That made them feel pretty good and just generally uplifted their spirit."

Irvin in the Negro Leagues

Irvin was a teenager when he first toured with the Newark Eagles in the summer of 1938, and he was in awe of the older players. "What impressed me was how the athletes looked. They looked like ballplayers," he wrote. "I liked the way their uniforms fit, the way they wore their cap, the fact that they showed a style in almost everything they did. It impressed me to want to become a professional baseball player." After a year-and-a-half-long stint at Lincoln University, where Irvin felt his talent was going to waste,

The Manleys' Unusual Scouting Tactics

Abe and Effa Manley went looking for the best baseball talent they could find—even if that meant finding it in prison! A warden in Miami wrote to Abe, telling him he had a prisoner named Fred Wilson who was an exceptional player. Wilson could be released as long as someone would assume responsibility for him. Abe Manley traveled to Florida to watch Wilson play in 1938 and signed him to the Eagles the very next season. Monte Irvin said Wilson was "the meanest man I've ever seen," but Wilson instantly liked Irvin and never gave him any trouble.

As Irvin said, "If you could survive on a team with Fred Wilson, you had to be doing something right."

this is exactly what he did. In 1938, Irvin began training with the Newark Eagles under the management of husband and wife Abe and Effa Manley. The Manleys were heroes of the early civil rights movement. They often put game proceeds toward ending the most vicious race crime of the times: lynching.

Lynchings were public murders carried out by angry mobs. African Americans were most often

Ray Dandridge

Ray Dandridge was one of the star players on the Newark Eagles when Monte Irvin joined the team. A talented third baseman and a great hitter, Dandridge was impossible to forget. "People would pay their way in to the game just to see him field," Irvin once said.

Dandridge started his professional career with the 1933 Detroit Stars and moved to the Eagles, for whom he starred throughout the remainder of the 1930s. He went to Mexico in 1940 and spent most of the decade there, even setting a Mexican league record for hitting safely in the most consecutive games. When he came back for a year in Newark in 1944, he batted .370, leading the Negro National League in hits, runs, and total bases.

In 1949, after Jackie Robinson signed with the Brooklyn Dodgers and broke the "color line," Dandridge was signed by the New York Giants and assigned to their Triple-A farm club at Minneapolis. He batted .363 his first year there, and won the league's MVP award in 1950, when he led Minneapolis to the league championship. Still, he never got promoted to the parent club. While at Minneapolis, Dandridge provided advice and assistance to a young Willie Mays, who went on to become a dazzling fielder.

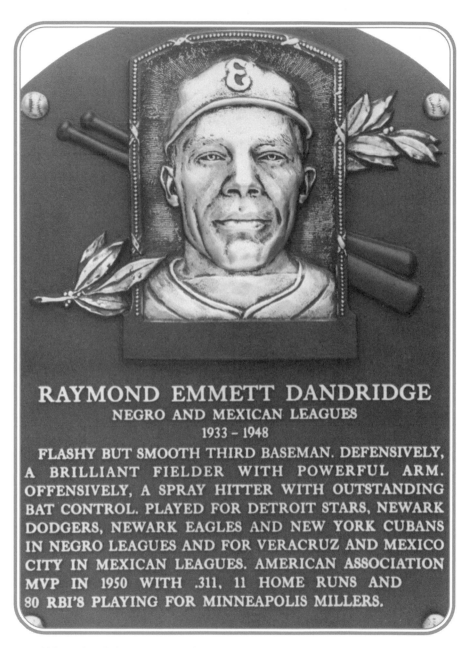

RAYMOND EMMETT DANDRIDGE
NEGRO AND MEXICAN LEAGUES
1933 – 1948
FLASHY BUT SMOOTH THIRD BASEMAN. DEFENSIVELY,
A BRILLIANT FIELDER WITH POWERFUL ARM.
OFFENSIVELY, A SPRAY HITTER WITH OUTSTANDING
BAT CONTROL. PLAYED FOR DETROIT STARS, NEWARK
DODGERS, NEWARK EAGLES AND NEW YORK CUBANS
IN NEGRO LEAGUES AND FOR VERACRUZ AND MEXICO
CITY IN MEXICAN LEAGUES. AMERICAN ASSOCIATION
MVP IN 1950 WITH .311, 11 HOME RUNS AND
80 RBI'S PLAYING FOR MINNEAPOLIS MILLERS.

Although celebrated Negro league third baseman Ray Dandridge
was signed by the New York Giants organization, he never made it
from the farm club to the big leagues.

The 1946 Newark Eagles, Negro league champions. Monte Irvin is on the far left in the back row.

the victims of lynchings, which were used as a method of intimidation to enforce Jim Crow laws. Between 1865 and 1965, thousands of African Americans were put to death by lynch mobs in southern states. Later investigations have shown that approximately one-third of all the victims were falsely accused. Most of the African Americans who were lynched had demanded civil rights, violated Jim Crow etiquette or laws,

Not only did Monte Irvin swing a powerful bat for the Newark Eagles during the 1930s and 1940s, he also carried a sure glove.

or fell victim to the aftermath of race riots. In fact, at least one-half of the lynchings were carried out with police officers participating.

In the 1938 baseball season, the Eagles had what everyone was calling a million-dollar infield, consisting of third baseman Ray Dandridge, Willie Wells at shortstop, Dick Seay at second base, and Mule Suttles on first. Irvin has said that Ray Dandridge was one of the best third basemen of all time. When former player and Los Angeles Dodgers manager Tommy Lasorda saw him play for the first time, Dandridge was already forty years old, but Lasorda said he had never seen a better fielding third baseman. Monte Irvin was proud to be part of such a talented group.

Hard Times
Hit Baseball

ong before Monte Irvin began to take the sport seriously, baseball was a fixture in the nation's consciousness.

All through the 1920s, Rube Foster's Negro National League thrived. Teams played a sixty- to eighty-game season, often drawing a crowd of 5,000 for weekend games; they all had a strong national following.

But in 1929, a shockwave was sent throughout the country that affected everyone. The stock market crash—now known as Black Friday—forced many able-bodied men out of work and many families became homeless. Farmers were hit hardest by the ensuing economic depression, but everyone was affected.

During the Great Depression, many displaced people set up shacks —now referred to as Depression shacks—on public lands, such as New York City's Central Park (shown here).

This period of economic hardship was a blow to the national pastime. At a time when most Americans couldn't afford the quarter admission to see a baseball game, attendance went down by nearly 40 percent. Some white ball players were nonetheless well paid: Babe Ruth earned $80,000 a season during the Depression. When asked how he felt about becoming so wealthy during an economic crisis that he commanded an even larger salary than U. S. President Herbert Hoover, Ruth famously quipped that, well, he'd had a better year than the president had!

During the worst of the Depression, Monte Irvin was a child living in New Jersey. His father worked long hours every day to bring home eighteen dollars a week to support the family. "Some people look at famous athletes as heroes, but men like my father are the real heroes to me," Irvin once said. Even though times were difficult, Irvin learned to love baseball by walking to the Grove Street Oval baseball park to watch the touring African American teams play. He said everyone set up folding chairs around the field and enjoyed some free entertainment.

Irvin was also lucky enough to have a father with a green thumb and a mother who was a whiz in the kitchen. The family grew all kinds of vegetables and fruit, enough to put food on their table and share with the neighbors, as well. Mary Eliza Irvin

Those hardest hit by the Depression—both young and old, frail and able—depended on soup kitchens for their meals.

canned the fruit and prepared wonderful meals that were famous with everyone in the community and, later, with Monte's ballplayer friends.

Not everyone was so industrious, and illegal gambling thrived in communities hit the hardest by the Depression. For only a few cents, anyone could place a bet by guessing the right three numbers that might result in a big win of six or seven dollars. Winning at "numbers" brought a little enjoyment into people's lives by allowing them an evening out on the town or a trip to the movies, but the gangsters who ran the numbers became instantly rich from their rackets. It was gangster money that helped revive baseball when it was down and out.

Original Gangsters

In the early 1920s, Gus Greenlee and his partner, Woogie Harris, controlled an illegal gambling racket in Pittsburgh. Greenlee's legitimate business, the Crawford Bar and Grille, was a front for the "numbers" games he ran. Numbers was very prominent throughout African American neighborhoods during the Depression. The game was played by choosing a three-digit number. If that number matched the number decided on for the day, the player won. The organizations that ran the numbers racket paid players on 500 to 1 odds, which meant that if you bet ten cents on your number, you could win up to fifty dollars.

The numbers eventually folded in Pittsburgh because an unusually large quantity of people chose the number 805 on one particular day. Since 805 was the number for the day, the organizers had to pay off a lot of people. This caused many of the racketeers to go broke, losing enough money to force them to retire.

Gus Greenlee was a Pittsburgh racketeer (gangster) who owned Greenlee's Crawford Bar and Grille, a dance hall in the heart of the African American section of Pittsburgh that regularly drew Duke Ellington, Lena Horne, Count Basie, and other jazz greats. He was also an active member of the African American community who wanted to promote his people. In 1930, he bought his town's local team, the Crawford Colored Giants, and two new seven-passenger cars to carry the team in style. Two years later, Greenlee bought the first entirely African American–owned stadium with $100,000 and named it Greenlee Field. By this time, Rube Foster's league was fully established, and now his top players had some fresh competition.

The Negro Leagues Thrive

Once Monte Irvin started playing for the Newark Eagles, he was earning $100 a month. This isn't a lot by today's standards, but consider what he points out in his autobiography: "At that time you could do a lot with a buck." Gas cost ten cents a gallon, and five dollars could feed a family of six for a week.

There is no disputing that Negro league players worked hard. African American players excelled under conditions that their white counterparts never had to deal with, including a longer season, much less pay, and a life spent more on the road than at home. Yet Irvin recalls these days on the road with fondness.

The Negro league season officially started in the deep South in February, with a spring training that usually lasted only a day, or perhaps a week. Then the players went on the road. Negro leaguers played so many games in so many places that they were said to "carry the news" from one African American community to another even more efficiently than the newspapers.

The big East-West all-star game at Comiskey Park in Chicago was the highlight of the season. Players were chosen by the fans themselves, who voted in the nation's two largest African American newspapers, the *Chicago Defender* and the *Pittsburgh Courier*. These weekly papers had a huge national readership: Pittsburgh's African American population didn't amount to more than 80,000 at the time, but the *Courier* had 277,000 readers nationwide. The paper's popularity

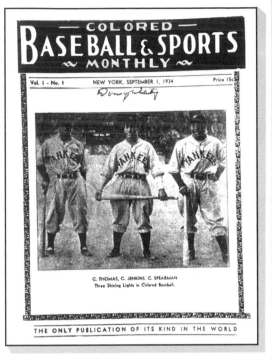

The popularity of Negro league baseball gave rise to a number of African American sports publications.

probably had as much to do with its coverage of African American sports as anything else.

The East-West tradition was started in 1933 by Gus Greenlee, and that first game turned out 20,000 fans. By the 1940s, over 50,000 fans of all races attended the all-star game. Although most of the spectators in the stands were African American, most sportswriters knew the event was too important to miss, and they covered it for big, national newspapers.

Negro League Baseball in the Jazz Age

Negro league players found themselves in the middle of a thriving culture of African American celebrity during the Jazz Age. Popular jazz, blues, and swing musicians supported the Negro league players along with the rest of the African American population.

Negro league baseball even made its way into popular music. "Did You See Jackie Robinson Hit That Ball?," a celebration of the player's greatness, was made famous by jazz big-band leader Count Basie's recording.

"Did you see Jackie Robinson hit that ball?

It went zoom in cross the left field wall.

Yeah boy, yes, yes. Jackie hit that ball.

And when he swung his bat, the crowd went wild,

because he knocked that ball a solid mile.

Yeah boy, yes, yes. Jackie hit that ball."

Monte Irvin played in four East-West games during his career with the Negro leagues, the first of which was in 1941. For him, major league all-star games weren't nearly as enjoyable as those in the Negro league. "The park would be decorated with red, white, and blue banners that had been put up everywhere, and a jazz band would play between innings," he wrote in his autobiography. "People like Count Basie, Ella Fitzgerald, and Billie Holiday would always make it their business to be in town for the East-West game, and we'd be sure to check them out at the jazz clubs. You didn't go to Chicago to sleep."

In fact, African American celebrities were great fans of the Negro leagues, and they often mingled with players when they found themselves in the same city. Jazz trumpeter Louis Armstrong regularly attended games, and the great tap dancer Bill "Bojangles" Robinson was even a part owner of one of the teams.

Each season ended with the Negro league World Series, but the playing didn't stop then for serious players like Irvin. All winter, many men continued playing off-season games in Florida in order to earn a living. As Homestead Grays star Buck Leonard said, "None of us made enough that we didn't have to work in the winter, not even Satchel Paige." One of the interesting things about the off-season was that African American and white players often competed together in special-attraction games as though it was not out of the ordinary.

Although African American players weren't earning enough money during the season to last them throughout the year, major league stars like Babe Ruth were becoming very wealthy. When the Babe signed a contract for $80,000 a season in 1930, the average Negro leaguer earned only about $200 a month. In addition, African American teams usually couldn't afford to pay a scorekeeper, so a lot of official information about player statistics and number of games was never recorded.

Like many African American entertainers of the time, tap dancer and actor Bill "Bojangles" Robinson was a great fan of the Negro leagues.

Life on the Road

Traveling from one small town to the next was no small task, either. Even though they were stars who often played for the entertainment of whites, Negro league players had to stick to the same segregation rules as the rest of the

country's African American people. After
playing three tough games in a day, it was not
uncommon for players to have to sleep on their
bus because no hotel in the area admitted
African Americans. Many restaurants they came
upon in their travels wouldn't let them in, or
they might have had to take a bath at a
sympathetic barber's shop for twenty-five cents.
Still, most players were hesitant to complain
about their careers. One Kansas City Monarch
has been quoted as saying: "We stayed in the
best hotels—they just happened to be black.
We ate in the best restaurants—they just
happened to be black-owned. Kansas City was
the Majors—it just happened to be black."

As the Newark Eagles traveled around the
country, Irvin and his teammates quickly became
much more sophisticated than the small-town
racism they encountered. In fact, Irvin says that
bigger cities nearly always had African American
establishments where the team could sleep or
eat. They sometimes received extra help from
good-hearted people who were sorry that

segregation laws made things so difficult. But they could count on having problems in rural areas or little villages in the Midwest, where sometimes the local residents had never seen an African American person before. In one rural spot in Mississippi, a service station attendant emptied all

Despite their popularity, Negro league players were subject to the segregation laws of the South.

the transmission fluid out of the Newark Eagles' bus when he was supposed to be changing the oil. The team discovered that a dirty trick had been played when their bus broke down later on the road.

Irvin didn't encounter too much racism personally and always dealt with people fairly.

Yet there was a racial incident that outraged African American players and fans alike. Jake Powell, outfielder for the New York Yankees, was quoted as saying that he liked to stay in shape during the off-season by "cracking niggers over the head." Yankee management responded to pressure from the African American press by suspending Powell and, amusingly, sending him on an apology tour of Harlem bars!

In the Negro leagues, sometimes the baseball itself was tougher. For one thing, pitchers often were not relieved by their coaches and had to pitch for nine innings straight. Players never left the game because of an injury. And it was said that African American players could hit anything because pitchers were allowed to get away with murder. Commonplace were spit balls, shine balls, and balls scuffed with a bottle cap to make them break more sharply. All of this made African American baseball exciting to watch. In fact, the Negro leagues turned bunting into an art form although it was scorned by the majors.

Best of the Negro League Teams

Atlanta Black Crackers, 1938

Atlantic City Bacharach Giants, 1926

Baltimore Black Sox, 1929

Baltimore Elite Giants, 1942

Birmingham Black Barons, 1943 team and 1948 team

Chicago American Giants, 1917 team, 1921 team, 1927 team, and 1933 team

Chicago Leland Giants, 1910

Cleveland Buckeyes, 1945

Detroit Stars, 1930

Harrisburg Giants, 1925

Hilldale Daisies, 1925

Homestead Grays, 1931 team, 1938 team, 1943 team, and 1948 team

Indianapolis ABCs, 1916

Kansas City Monarchs, 1924 team, 1929 team, 1942 team, and 1946 team

Memphis Red Sox, 1938

Newark Eagles, 1937 team and 1946 team

New York Lincoln Giants, 1913 team and 1930 team

New York Cubans, 1947

Philadelphia Stars, 1934

Pittsburgh Crawfords, 1932 team and 1935 team

St. Louis Stars, 1930

Courtesy of blackbaseball.com

Kansas City Monarch Satchel Paige prepares to bunt a ball during a Negro league game.

The hard-scrabble Negro leagues influenced major league baseball in other ways. Because they had to squeeze so many games into a season, the Kansas City Monarchs began transporting bright lights on their buses to allow them to play in the dark. Thus, the birth of night baseball.

Highlights and Struggles in the Negro Leagues

Negro league baseball was a truly exciting game. The players had so much talent to spare that they got creative to make things interesting. Flashy plays in the infield and outfield and daring moves like bunting and base stealing that didn't turn up often in the majors were commonplace in the Negro Leagues.

Monte Irvin really began to come into his own as a player in 1941, when he played in his first East-West all-star game in Chicago's Comiskey Park. These games were the highlight of the Negro league season and, in some ways, a highlight of African American culture. African American baseball fans traveled from all over

Fans of Negro league baseball were often mesmerized by the razzle-dazzle style of play by many of its stars.

the country to see the players they had selected with their votes.

The all-star competition was more than just a baseball game. Monte Irvin said in his autobiography that those games gave all African Americans some hope for their future: If African American baseball players could excel under such tough conditions, surely they could succeed, too.

Monte Irvin's Major League Batting Statistics

Year	Team	Games	At-Bat	Runs	Hits	TB	2B	3B	HR	RBI
1949	NYG	36	76	7	17	24	3	2	0	7
1950	NYG	110	374	61	112	186	19	5	15	66
1951	NYG	151	558	94	174	287	19	11	24	121
1952	NYG	46	126	10	39	55	2	1	4	21
1953	NYG	124	444	72	146	240	21	5	21	97
1954	NYG	135	432	62	113	189	13	3	19	64
1955	NYG	51	150	16	38	50	7	1	1	17
1956	CHI	111	339	44	92	156	13	3	15	50
Total	8 years	764	2499	366	731	1187	97	31	99	443

SH	SF	SB	CS	BB	IBB	HBP	Strike Outs	Batting Average	SLG.	On Base %
0	0	0	0	17	0	0	11	.224	.316	.366
1	0	3	0	52	0	5	41	.299	.497	.392
1	0	12	2	89	0	9	44	.312	.514	.415
0	0	0	1	10	0	1	11	.310	.437	.365
0	0	2	0	55	0	3	34	.329	.541	.406
3	5	7	4	70	0	2	23	.262	.437	.363
1	2	3	0	17	0	3	15	.253	.333	.337
3	4	1	0	41	5	0	41	.271	.460	.346
9	11	28	7	351	5	23	220	.293	.475	.383

Winter Leagues

One of the major downsides of being shut out of the majors was that the Negro leaguers could never be sure if they were major league–caliber players. However well he competed, Irvin couldn't use the majors as a measuring stick without facing those players. Sure enough, when

In a display of lightning-fast speed and sheer audacity, New York Giant Monte Irvin steals home from third base in the first inning of the 1951 World Series against the New York Yankees.

Irvin traveled to San Juan, Puerto Rico, he and the other players learned firsthand that they were as skilled as their white teammates.

Irvin and lots of other Negro leaguers had positive experiences playing for the Caribbean leagues. These countries did not enforce the type of race restrictions that existed in the United States, and in fact many of the best Cuban players were African American.

Irvin enjoyed his brief time in Puerto Rico, especially the tournament at the end of the winter season between teams from Cuba, Santo Domingo, and San Juan. Puerto Rican baseball fans were completely in awe of Irvin's fantastic throwing arm.

Soon after, Irvin also spent a season with the Mexican league. His decision to go to Mexico to play was motivated in large part by money. In fact, quite a few Negro league teams suffered because of the winter leagues: Many players were lured down to the Caribbean and Mexico for better money and, in some ways, a better life.

By 1942, Irvin had established himself as one of the best players in the whole league, batting well over .500. Renowned Mexican manager Jorge Pasquel sent him a telegram offering a much higher salary: $500 a month, compared to the $150 he received from the Eagles. His manager, Effa Manley, wouldn't match the price, so Irvin married his fiancee, Dee, and they both trekked down to Mexico.

The Vera Cruz Blues and all the other Mexican teams were doing exceptionally well that season, and Irvin attributed their success to all the great African American players who had come down to play. "It was just a terrific year for me in every way," he raved in his autobiography, describing a typical Sunday that started with a ten o'clock game with time left over to take in a bullfight the same afternoon. He was on his honeymoon, he played the best year of baseball of his life, and he enjoyed Mexico City, all new from being rebuilt after a recent earthquake. Irvin had every intention of heading back to Mexico the following year, but World War II changed everything.

Monte Irvin's Major League Fielding Statistics

Career Fielding Statistics

Year	Pos	Team	G	PO	A	E	DP	PCT
1949	OF	NYG	10	15	3	0	0	1.000
1949	1B	NYG	5	40	3	0	5	1.000
1949	3B	NYG	5	1	11	1	1	.923
1950	OF	NYG	49	109	2	1	0	.991
1950	1B	NYG	59	459	48	11	62	.979
1950	3B	NYG	1	1	1	0	0	1.000
1951	OF	NYG	112	237	10	1	1	.996
1951	1B	NYG	39	348	50	8	47	.980
1952	OF	NYG	32	44	3	0	1	1.000
1953	OF	NYG	113	244	10	7	4	.973
1954	OF	NYG	128	274	7	7	0	.976
1954	1B	NYG	1	2	0	0	0	1.000
1954	3B	NYG	1	0	0	1	0	.000
1955	OF	NYG	45	94	4	4	0	.961
1956	OF	CHI	96	216	6	2	0	.991
Overall Total			696	2084	158	43	121	.981

Putting His Career on Hold

Like all Americans living during World War II, Monte Irvin could recall the time he heard about the bombing at Pearl Harbor as though it were yesterday. He was on the field in Puerto Rico and had just hit a double when an announcement came over the loudspeaker that Japan had attacked the United States' major port in Hawaii. The United States had declared war in return. The Puerto Rican fans in the stands cheered the announcement, but Irvin says he was struck by the hardship this war was sure to bring—at home, on the island of Puerto Rico, and in his own life.

Sure enough, Irvin was drafted to fight in the war nearly two years later. He was assigned to an all–African American engineering outfit, and served his tour of duty in England, France, and Germany. Irvin didn't want to leave his baseball career or his wife and five-month-old daughter behind, but he didn't have a choice. Overseas, his outfit built bridges and roads and did guard duty.

When the war ended, Irvin returned to Puerto Rico to get back into the game. "After

Irvin's baseball career was interrupted when the United States entered World War II after the Japanese attack on Pearl Harbor.

I came out of service, I was never the same guy that I was when I went in," he wrote in his autobiography. "I had lost my timing, and I was three years older. Right away, I realized that I had lost something and I worked hard trying to come back." He played for the San Juan Senadores and got ready for his next big challenge: the 1946 Negro league World Series.

Monte Irvin's Career Highlights

Height: 6' 1" Weight: 195 lbs.

Batted: Right

Threw: Right

Position: Outfield (also, third base and first base)

He was a four-sport high school star in New Jersey before he turned pro when he was seventeen.

During the next ten years in the Negro leagues, it was estimated that he had a batting average of .350.

In one season in the Mexican league, he batted .397 and was named the MVP.

In only eight years in the major leagues, he collected 731 hits.

He had a career batting average in the National League of .293.

In the 1951 World Series he hit .458 for New York, slugging 11 hits in 24 at-bats.

His best year in the majors was 1951, when he hit .312, hit 24 home runs, drove in a league leading 121 runs, and scored 94 runs.

He was inducted into the Baseball Hall of Fame in 1973.

Highlights courtesy of the official Web site for Monte Irvin, www.cmgww.com/baseball/irvin/micare.html

The End of an Era

For eighty years—nearly the entire lifespan of professional baseball—African American players had been excluded from playing with whites in the major leagues. Around the middle of the twentieth century, after World War II, the racial climate in America began to change. In fact, many sportswriters who had long been in favor of integrating baseball used the war as a playing card, arguing of Negro league players, "If he's good enough for the navy, he's good enough for the majors."

In 1945, Judge Kenesaw Mountain Landis died, leaving vacant the position of baseball commissioner and clearing the way for integrated

Baseball commissioner Kenesaw Mountain Landis *(right)*, who opposed the integration of major league baseball, poses with National League president John Heydler after a league meeting in the early 1940s.

baseball. Landis was a federal judge when he became Major League Baseball's first commissioner in 1920, and he was known for ruling his new athletic jurisdiction with an iron fist. He had been completely against the idea of African Americans and whites playing together in the major leagues. With Landis gone, Branch Rickey, president and general manager of the Brooklyn Dodgers, went up against the "gentleman's agreement" that existed to keep African American players out of the majors.

Even before World War II, people were calling to integrate major league baseball. In a 1938 poll of major leaguers, four out of five had said they would have no problem playing with and against African Americans. And for a few years, many sportswriters had penned articles condemning the racism of the major leagues. Chester Washington of the *Pittsburgh Courier* even sent a telegram to the manager of the Pittsburgh Pirates. The Pirates were struggling, and Washington suggested he look into the abundance of talent in the Negro leagues. He received no answer.

"If I had been the first one chosen, I think I could have done the job because all you had to do was play. I grew up in an integrated situation, where I played sports in grade school and high school with white teammates. I never had any problem. I didn't care about skin color, and I think I had the type of personality to handle any situation . . . But, again, so could those other fellows."

—Monte Irvin, *Nice Guys Finish First*

Branch Rickey was quite a character, one of the many colorful people to play a part in baseball lore. Known fondly as "The Mahatma," he took a serious and nearly religious approach to managing baseball. He was famous for his ability to make smart trades and had an eye for a lot of important changes on baseball's horizon. For instance, he was a champion of new additions to the game such as batting cages, pitching machines, batting helmets, and a string outline of the strike zone rigged over home plate for pitchers working on control. His eye for talent inevitably led him to break the color barrier in modern professional baseball. Scouting the Negro leagues for the best talent, Rickey had earmarked Monte Irvin as the

Effa Manley, co-owner of the Newark Eagles, cheers her team during a game against the New York Black Yankees.

Effa Manley

Effa Manley, co-owner of the Newark Eagles, was born in Philadelphia in 1900, the child of an extramarital (outside a marriage) affair between Bertha Ford Brooks and financier John M. Bishop. All of Manley's half-brothers and half-sisters were the result of previous marriages and were one-half African American. Manley's mother and father were both white, but she chose to identify as an African American. In 1932, she met Abe Manley, they eventually married, and three years later the husband-and-wife team bought the Newark Eagles.

The Manleys lived in Sugar Hill, an upper-class section of Harlem that included such residents as W. E. B. Du Bois, civil rights activist Roy Wilkins, novelist Walter White, and Thurgood Marshall, the first African American Supreme Court Justice. Effa Manley was a social activist; her service included work on the Children's Day Camp Committee and the community-organized Citizen's League for Fair Play. The Citizen's League organized a 1934 boycott of white-owned Harlem stores that refused to hire African American salesclerks. Manley walked in the picket lines and negotiated the hiring of African Americans for better jobs than the menial labor that was available to them. She was also treasurer of the Newark NAACP.

Manley also used her high-profile status as a Negro league manager to rail against the biggest crime against civil rights of the day. Her famous "Anti-Lynching Days" at the ballpark brought in a lot of fans, and she directed the proceeds of these games toward the social movement.

"I constantly look at my scrapbook," Manley once said. "That scrapbook is fascinating. People say 'Don't live in the past.' But I guess it depends on how interesting your past is."

Effa Manley died in 1981, the only woman to have actively managed an all-male professional baseball team.

first to make the switch to the majors. But World War II came calling, making other plans for Irvin.

Integration into the Major Leagues

What happened next is a major moment in African American history, in baseball history, and in American history. In 1945, Jackie Robinson, second baseman for the Kansas City Monarchs, was spotted by one of Branch Rickey's scouts and chosen to be the first African American man to play in the major leagues. The decision was called baseball's "Great Experiment" of integration. Robinson went on to be the first African American player to win the MVP (most valuable player) award, to be inducted into the Baseball Hall of Fame, and to be named Rookie of the Year. He was also the first baseball player of any race to have his face on a U.S. postage stamp. A figure loved and lauded by sports fans of all backgrounds, Robinson had an influence on American culture that cannot be overstated.

Jackie Robinson broke major league baseball's color barrier
when he joined the Brooklyn Dodgers in 1945. Even more than
his athletic talent, his ability to deal with racism was critical to the
success of integrated baseball.

Branch Rickey himself called Robinson the most competitive player since the great Ty Cobb. Robinson had a lot in common with Monte Irvin, including his all-around athletic talent. He was the first student athlete at UCLA to earn four varsity letters, and he was called by his coaches both the best football and the best basketball player they had seen.

Hoping that racial tensions would be less severe in Canada, Rickey started Robinson out in the International League in Montreal before adding him to the Brooklyn Dodgers' lineup. As expected, Robinson took some hard knocks in exchange for the honor of being the first African American in the majors. Yet his great achievement was believed by some to be an accident of fate. Effa Manley later told Monte Irvin that she had selected him to be the one to go on to the majors, but it didn't work out that way. Irvin was drafted to fight in World War II, and when he got back he was older and not the player he'd been at twenty. "Most of the African American ball players thought Monte Irvin should have been the first African American ball player in the major leagues," Negro leaguer Cool Papa Bell later said. "Monte was our best young ball player at the time. He could hit that long ball, he had a great arm and he could field and run. He could do everything."

Although Irvin wasn't the first to cross the color line, he ended up having a very successful tenure in the major leagues. He would soon be signed to the New York Giants.

When Jackie Robinson joined the major leagues, African American baseball spectators all over the country became loyal Dodgers fans overnight. And they supported integration with their pocketbooks by attending all the games that featured their new hero. When Effa Manley complained that attendance to Negro league games had dropped off sharply, she was criticized by some who held integration as the height of African American achievement.

Not surprisingly, Negro league managers were not suitably paid for the players they traded to the major leagues. Effa Manley felt stiffed by the Giants when they pulled Monte Irvin over to the other side of the color line.

The Negro leagues began to lose their juice just a few years after Jackie Robinson introduced America to the idea of racially integrated baseball. Following the 1948 season the Negro National League closed up shop, but African American teams did continue to play for several years. Integration did not happen overnight, and many Negro league players who had been denied the chance to play in the big leagues never lost their loyalty to the teams that made them. Yet the overall talent of the teams that continued to play gradually declined as the younger players were courted by major league franchises.

A Good Deal

When Abe and Effa Manley accepted a $5,000 deal from the Giants for Monte Irvin's contract, they received only $1,000. Effa treated herself to a mink stole with some of the money and wore it for years. She wore the stole at a Negro leagues reunion in Kentucky more than thirty years later. Irvin complimented her on it, saying, "You made a good buy, Mrs. Manley." "Not as good as the Giants did," she replied.

Years later, a 1957 article in the *Sporting News* would report that African American baseball was still struggling to be a presence in the sports world. J. B. Martin, the president of the Negro American League, who served his post for no salary, said he was keeping the league alive as a way to train African American players for the big leagues.

Certainly, integration of the majors led to the demise of the Negro leagues. But the *Sporting News* article pointed to several factors that contributed to the decline in its popularity, such as the improved economic state of African Americans, the accessibility of television, and the draw of other sports.

Within a year, Negro baseball had lost its relevance—to the great disappointment of some and the relief of others. A reaction to legalized racism, the league had nonetheless been a source of pride and hope for the African American community.

The Major Leagues and Beyond

Even though Monte Irvin believed he could never again be the brilliant player he'd been at twenty, he came back from the war and practiced hard and took good care of himself. Jackie Robinson had already been signed to the Dodgers, taking away Irvin's chance to be the first African American player in the majors, but Irvin patiently awaited his turn. He returned to the Eagles in 1947 and watched his teammate Larry Doby get scouted out for the Cleveland Indians, making him the first African American player in the American League.

Irvin was puzzled that major league team owners still seemed slow to discover the rich

Monte Irvin *(left)* visits **Jackie Robinson** in the Dodgers' dressing room after a World Series game between the Brooklyn Dodgers and the New York Yankees.

resources Negro league teams had to offer. Still, he knew his dedication would pay off eventually. Sure enough, in 1948 Clyde Sukeforth, the same scout who had spotted Robinson, offered Irvin a contract with the Dodgers. Due to quibbles over money, the contract was dropped. However, when Irvin was thirty the Giants signed him, and he said that it was the best thing that ever happened to him.

Irvin said he tried to make three primary adjustments during the transition to the majors. The first was tuning up to be the best player he could be. The second was getting used to not being the very top player. Quite simply, Irvin had always been the best at everything in baseball that he'd put his mind to: his arm couldn't be beat, he was great in the field, and he was exceptionally fast. Now, he was competing against the cream of the crop and he was no longer at the top of his game. The third adjustment was getting used to the level of organization in the majors. Not that this was a bad thing: Irvin was delighted to find that

Baseball Hall of Fame

"Annual attendance at the Baseball Hall of Fame and Museum in Cooperstown, New York, regularly approaches 350,000 and twice has topped 400,000. The shrine is open year-round, and during July and August it is not unusual for the daily turnstile count to exceed Cooperstown's population."

—www.baseballhalloffame.org

Baseball fans at the Baseball Hall of Fame and Museum view the plaques celebrating the accomplishments of baseball players who have been inducted into the Hall of Fame.

someone had the job of handling the players' equipment and uniforms. In the Negro leagues, those details had been the individual responsibility of each player.

Negro leaguers had certain advantages over their white counterparts in the majors, according to Irvin. While players in the Negro leagues had seen many major league games, white players had mostly ignored African American baseball and often had no idea what they were up against. Because of the myth that African American baseball was somehow unorganized and sloppy, many white players believed that African Americans couldn't make it in the majors. Of course, they were wrong.

First Robinson, then Doby, Irvin, and those who followed, proved themselves as good as any player in the majors. And while Jackie Robinson had a well-documented tough time with the tense racial situation, Irvin and fellow Negro league player Hank Thompson slid into the camaraderie of the Giants with few problems. There was a certain uneasiness about the new

Monte Irvin makes a spectacular catch during a World Series game against the New York Yankees in 1951.

situation, but most of the guys were warm and welcoming to Irvin. Yet when the Giants went to Arizona for training, Irvin experienced much of the same racism and segregation he remembered from the old days traveling in the South. Soon thereafter, Willie Mays joined the team, and his talent and charisma went a long way in smoothing over those ripples.

While he played for the Giants, Irvin had several memorable experiences. In 1949, he made a throw against the St. Louis Cardinals that sportswriter Bob Broeg claimed cost the Cardinals the pennant.

But the peak of all of Irvin's exciting moments as a major league ballplayer was stealing home in the 1951 World Series against the New York Yankees. The feat hadn't been done in thirty years, and it delighted the crowd and embarrassed the Yankees. The two years that the Giants took the pennant—1951 and 1953—were Irvin's best seasons.

His last year with the Giants was 1955. Although he was playing well, he did not

Bowie Kuhn, shown here formally inducting Hank Aaron into the Baseball Hall of Fame in 1982, developed a close friendship with Monte Irvin after Irvin was appointed as a special assistant to the commissioner in 1968, when Kuhn was an attorney for the National League.

bounce back from an injured ankle as successfully as he would have liked. He was surprised when the Giants sent him down to play with the Cubs farm club in Minneapolis. The Cubs picked up Irvin the following year, and he stayed with the team until he was thirty-seven. From there, he went to the Los Angeles Angels in the Pacific Coast League, but retired from the sport entirely in 1957, when he began to have back problems.

Life After Baseball

As a retired ballplayer, Monte Irvin still had interesting experiences ahead of him. He went to work full-time for the Rheingold Brewing Company as a regional representative. This job led him to work with Jackie Robinson, who did a few endorsements for the company.

But one of Irvin's most important post-baseball appointments was working as special assistant to the commissioner in 1968. There, he had the opportunity to work with Bowie

Kuhn, who was the attorney for the National League. The two became great friends and worked well as a team until they retired together sixteen years later. The job was not always easy, though—baseball had changed. There were a lot of disagreements to be settled, including players who were operating as free agents, strikes, and other disputes. Irvin's sense of fair play and level-headedness served him well in his position.

One of his responsibilities was to set up entertainment for the World Series each year. He was excited to get the Jackson Five to sing the national anthem one year when no one else he worked with had even heard of them! His job looked like it might be in jeopardy, but needless to say the group performed to a standing ovation and went on to become a huge success.

The Baseball Hall of Fame

The Baseball Hall of Fame opened in Cooperstown, New York, in 1939 to much

The Negro Leagues Baseball Museum

The men who played for the Negro leagues have been honored in a museum. The Negro Leagues Baseball Museum in Kansas City, Missouri, opened in January 1991 and includes information about and memorabilia from the Negro leagues' heyday.

Twelve of the stars of Negro league baseball have been immortalized with life-sized bronze sculptures. The museum also features film and video exhibits, interactive computer stations, a gallery, and the Double Play Action Center, a sports entertainment showcase. There, visitors can try their hand at the Power Alley Interactive Batting System, a high-tech simulator that allows patrons to go up against the best pitchers in the major leagues today.

The museums at 18th and Vine Street in Kansas City, Missouri, include the Negro Leagues Baseball Museum and the American Jazz Museum.

fanfare. At that time, there were still no African Americans in the majors, and it would be many years before the most prominent Negro league players were recognized for all their hard work.

Bowie Kuhn worked hard to set up the Negro League Committee at the Hall of Fame. But Irvin says the formation of the committee was originally due to an off-hand remark made by his buddy Roy Campanella one day. When asked how many Negro leaguers he felt had been of Hall of Fame quality, he replied, "Oh, three or four." This was all the encouragement the commissioner needed to set up the special Negro League Committee.

The group put many hours of thought and discussion toward deciding which former Negro league players were deserving of consideration for the Hall of Fame. Ultimately, thirty men were selected. This caused a bit of a commotion, particularly with those who resisted the idea of Negro league players joining the Hall of Fame in the first place. Later, Campanella explained that he was erring on the

Satchel Paige chats with ex–Brooklyn Dodger Roy Campanella before major league baseball's all-star game at Yankee Stadium on August 20, 1961.

side of caution when he suggested just a handful of Negro league players; he was afraid of scaring off the organizers by suggesting a larger number and losing his chance altogether.

Back in the commissioner's office, Irvin was made chairman of the selection committee. Then, beginning in 1969 with Satchel Paige, a select group of Negro leaguers were inducted into the Hall of Fame. By 1982, nine former Negro leaguers (as well as Rube Foster) had been inducted, including Monte Irvin himself.

Irvin's name entered the Hall of Fame in 1973. He was inducted along with four others, including his former apprentice, the late Roberto Clemente, with whom he had played in Puerto Rico. Clemente's widow accepted the honor on Roberto's behalf, as he had been killed only months earlier in a plane crash. Irvin says he will never forget that day.

Irvin was also honored by President George Bush in 1992, himself a big baseball fan and a former college athlete. As part of an African American history month celebration, Monte

MONFORD (MONTE) IRVIN
NEGRO LEAGUES 1937-1948
NEW YORK N.L., CHICAGO N.L.,
1949-1956
REGARDED AS ONE OF NEGRO LEAGUES' BEST
HITTERS. STAR SLUGGER OF NEWARK EAGLES
WON 1946 NEGRO LEAGUE BATTING TITLE.
LED N.L. IN RUNS BATTED IN AND PACED
"MIRACLE" GIANTS IN HITTING IN 1951
DRIVE TO PENNANT. BATTED .458 AND
STOLE HOME IN 1951 WORLD SERIES.

ROBERTO WALKER CLEMENTE
PITTSBURGH N. L. 1955-1972
MEMBER OF EXCLUSIVE 3,000-HIT CLUB. LED
NATIONAL LEAGUE IN BATTING FOUR TIMES.
HAD FOUR SEASONS WITH 200 OR MORE HITS
WHILE POSTING LIFETIME .317 AVERAGE AND
240 HOME RUNS. WON MOST VALUABLE PLAYER
AWARD 1966. RIFLE-ARMED DEFENSIVE STAR
SET N.L. MARK BY PACING OUTFIELDERS IN
ASSISTS FIVE YEARS. BATTED .362 IN TWO
WORLD SERIES, HITTING IN ALL 14 GAMES.

Monte Irvin's plaque rests beside Roberto Clemente's on the walls of the Baseball Hall of Fame. They were both inducted on August 6, 1973.

Irvin, Leon Day, Jimmy Crutchfield, and Josh Gibson Jr. were invited to the East Room of the White House for a personal reception with the president.

The face of professional baseball and the Hall of Fame have changed dramatically during Monte Irvin's lifetime. When Irvin was a teenager just learning to love the game, his

Although he finally made it to the major leagues, it was Monte Irvin's accomplishments in the Negro leagues that secured his place in baseball's Hall of Fame.

highest aspiration was the Negro leagues, which was the best an African American player could hope for at that time. He is proud of his work in the Negro leagues and grateful to live during a time when he could see things change for the better. Irvin only wishes his fellow African American baseball players who never got to try their hand at the majors had received the recognition they deserved.

Monte Irvin had left his hometown of Haleburg, Alabama, angry at the injustices against African Americans. He rose above these limitations and many more, making him a true American hero.

Timeline

1896 Supreme Court rules in *Plessy v. Ferguson* that African Americans and whites should maintain "separate but equal" existences.

1919 Monte Irvin born in Haleburg, Alabama.

1919 Negro National League formed by Rube Foster.

1923 Ed Bolden founds the Eastern Colored League.

1927 The Irvin family moves north to New Jersey.

1936 Monte Irvin joins the Newark Eagles.

1942 Irvin is drafted to fight in World War II.

1949 Irvin joins the major leagues, playing for the New York Giants.

1956 Irvin injures his ankle and is drafted to the Minneapolis Cubs.

1957 Irvin retires from professional baseball.

1968 Irvin is appointed to position of special assistant to the commissioner.

1973 Irvin is inducted into the Baseball Hall of Fame.

Glossary

discrimination To treat someone badly simply because of his or her gender, race, or class.

franchise A professional sports team.

free agent Athlete who is free to sign a contract with any team.

injustice Violation of the rights of another.

integrate To bring parts together, as with African Americans and whites.

Jim Crow law The practice of discriminating against and segregating African Americans.

lynching A murder, usually a hanging, by a mob.

numbers A form of gambling.

racism The belief that one race is superior to others.

racketeer A person who conducts illegal business activities.

RBI (Run Batted In) A statistic given to a batter for causing a run to score.

segregation Separating people of different races.

submission Surrendering.

For More Information

National Baseball Hall of Fame and Museum
25 Main Street
P.O. Box 590
Cooperstown, NY 13326
(888) HALL-OF-FAME (425-5633)
Web site: http://www.baseballhalloffame.org

Negro Leagues Baseball Museum
1616 East 18th Street
Kansas City, MO 64108-1610
(816) 221-1920
Web site: http://www.nlbm.com

In Canada

Canadian Baseball Hall of Fame Museum
386 Church Street
St. Marys, ON N4X 1C2
(877) 250-2255
(519) 284-1838
Web site: http://www.baseballhof.ca

Web Sites

The Baseball Archive
http://www.baseball1.com/

Baseball History—Negro League
http://www.baseballhistory.com/
    negroleaguemain.asp

Baseball Library—Monte Irvin Biography
http://sportsline.com/u/baseball/bol/sabr/tbi/I/
    Irvin_Monte.tbi.html

Black Baseball
http://www.blackbaseball.com

Major League Baseball History and Statistics
http://www.baseball-reference.com

Monte Irvin Official Site
http://www.cmgww.com/baseball/irvin/
micare.html

Negro League Baseball
http://www.negroleaguebaseball.com/

Videos
Baseball—A Film by Ken Burns, 1994.

Soul of the Game, 1996, directed by Kevin
Rodney Sullivan.

*There Was Always Sun Shining Someplace: Life
in the Negro Baseball Leagues,* 1984, directed
by Craig Davidson.

For Further Reading

Cooper, Michael L. *Playing America's Game: The Story of Negro League Baseball.* New York: Lodestar Books, 1993.

Irvin, Monte, and James A. Riley. *Nice Guys Finish First: The Autobiography of Monte Irvin.* New York: Carroll & Graf, 1996.

Margolies, Jacob. *The Negro Leagues: The Story of Black Baseball.* New York: Franklin Watts, 1993.

Ribowsky, Mark. *A Complete History of the Negro Leagues, 1884 to 1955.* Secaucus, NJ: Carol Publishing Group, 1997.

Ritter, Lawrence S. *Leagues Apart: The Men and Times of the Negro Baseball Leagues.* New York: Morrow Junior Books, 1999.

Ward, Geoffrey C., Ken Burns, and Jim
    O'Connor. *Shadow Ball: The History of the
    Negro Leagues.* New York: Knopf, 1994.
Winter, Jonah. *Fair Ball! 14 Great Stars from
    Baseball's Negro Leagues.* New York:
    Scholastic Press, 1999.

Index

About the Author

Katie Haegele is a Philadelphia-based writer and editor.

Photo Credits

Cover and pp. 6, 12, 16, 20, 43, 45, 55, 69, 75, 78, 84, 86, 88, 90, 95, 97, 98 © Corbis; pp. 4, 25, 38, 39, 64, 93 © AP/Wide World Photos; pp. 19, 32, 40, 49, 58 © New York Public Library; p. 28 © Library of Congress; pp. 34, 53, 61, 72 © Hulton Archive.

Layout

Nelson Sá

Design

Claudia Carlson